JOEY LOGANO

BY MARY BLECKWEHL

AMICUS LEARNING

Inspire is published by
Amicus Learning, an imprint of Amicus
P.O. Box 227
Mankato, MN 56002
www.amicuspublishing.us

Editor: Ana Brauer
Series Designer: Kathleen Petelinsek
Book Designer and Photo Researcher: Emily Dietz

Library of Congress Cataloging-in-Publication Data
Names: Bleckwehl, Mary E., author.
Title: Joey Logano / by Mary Bleckwehl.
Description: Mankato, MN : Amicus Learning, 2026. | Series: Inspire | Includes bibliographical references and index. | Audience: Ages 5–9 | Audience: Grades 2–3 | Summary: "Learn about NASCAR driver Joey Logano and his accomplishments in an engaging profile packed with photos and fact-filled text suitable for young readers. Includes table of contents, glossary, further resources, and index"— Provided by publisher.
Identifiers: LCCN 2024044111 (print) | LCCN 2024044112 (ebook) | ISBN 9798892005180 (library binding) | ISBN 9798892005722 (paperback) | ISBN 9798892006262 (ebook)
Subjects: LCSH: Logano, Joey, 1990—Juvenile literature. | Stock car drivers—United States—Biography—Juvenile literature.
Classification: LCC GV1032.L65 B54 2026 (print) | LCC GV1032.L65 (ebook) | DDC 796.72092 [B]—dc23/eng/20241124
LC record available at https://lccn.loc.gov/2024044111
LC ebook record available at https://lccn.loc.gov/2024044112

Photo Credits: Associated Press/Keith Gillett/Icon Sportswire, cover, Terry Renna, 6; Getty Images/Andy Lyons, 11, Chris Trotman, 15, Darrell Ingham, 9, David Rosenblum/Icon Sportswire, 18–19, Jared C. Tilton, 20, Jonathan Ferrey, 16–17, Sean Gardner, 5, 21, Streeter Lecka, 13, Wesley Hitt, 12–13; Shutterstock/Bruce Alan Bennett, 7, sripfoto, 8

Table of Contents

Master of the Speedway

The wild 300-lap race is in overtime. No. 22 leads in the last lap. But the engine sputters. It's running out of gas! The driver **drifts** to keep cars from passing. Professional **NASCAR** driver Joey Logano roars to the finish line. Victory!

Joey Logano has driven number 22 for Team Penske since 2013.

Logano knew he wanted to be a stock car driver from a young age.

Bit by the Racing Bug

If it had wheels, young Logano loved it. He raced Hot Wheels, Power Wheels, and his favorite, a go-kart. By age seven he was racing quarter midget cars. He won a championship title three years in a row.

SAFE RACING

Quarter midget cars look like go-karts with a roll cage. They can reach speeds of 30–50 mph (48–80 km/h).

Logano became a development driver in 2005. This means he trained to drive race cars.

Off to the Races

Logano was **competitive** and liked winning. At nine, he began racing **Legends** cars. He was the youngest racer. At age 12, he had 14 wins in a row at Atlanta Motor Speedway. This was a record.

NICKNAME

Logano's nickname is "Sliced Bread." NASCAR driver Randy LaJoie said young Logano would be the best thing since sliced bread.

ATLANTA
MOTOR SPEEDWAY

The Big Break to NASCAR

Logano's NASCAR **debut** came in 2008, just after his 18th birthday. In his third race, he won at Kentucky Speedway. This made him the youngest winner in the Nationwide Series. A year later, he earned NASCAR Cup Series Rookie of the Year.

Logano started his NASCAR career in 2008 with Joe Gibbs Racing.

Logano says Mark Martin helped him become a better racer.

The Real Deal

Mark Martin is a NASCAR Hall of Famer. He was Logano's childhood hero. Martin saw ten-year-old Logano beat experienced racers. Martin called him "the real deal." Martin became his racing **mentor**.

RACING HERO

In 2012, Logano raced against Mark Martin. Logano won! He beat Martin by 0.997 seconds.

A Second Chance

Logano hit a rocky racing patch. He got fired by his racing team. But he got a second chance. Team Penske picked him to drive No. 22 in 2013. Logano qualified for NASCAR playoffs his first year. Then came his biggest season. He made five trips to **Victory Lane** in 2014.

DID YOU KNOW?
Logano only won two races during his time with Joe Gibbs Racing.

Switching to Team Penske allowed Logano to shine as a driver.

The Great American Race

The Daytona 500 is a 500-mile (805-kilometer) race. It is the most important race in NASCAR.

In 2015, Logano sat fifth in the Daytona 500 lineup. The green flag dropped. Cars roared to life. For 31 of the 203 laps, No. 22 led. When Logano crossed the finish line, the checkered flag was his. He won the Great American Race!

Logano greets fans during the Daytona 500 in Florida.

Off the Track

Logano loves winning. That includes seeing others do well. The Joey Logano Foundation gives a second chance to those in need. Filling backpacks and helping build homes are just two ways his charity helps.

A HAIRY CONNECTION

Logano has alopecia, a hair loss condition. His foundation helps families learn about hair loss solutions.

PENNZOIL
Shell
500
DAYTONA

Logano is one of 10 drivers who have won three or more championships.

Future of a Speed Champion

Joey Logano is one of NASCAR's biggest winners. He has over 30 Cup wins. He won the NASCAR Cup Series championship in 2018, 2022, and 2024. But his racing story is not over! Every race is his chance to win again.

DID YOU KNOW?

In 2024, Logano won the Wild Ally 400 at Nashville Superspeedway. The race had a record five overtimes.

SUPER STATS

JOSEPH THOMAS LOGANO

Birthday: May 24, 1990

Birthplace: Middletown, Connecticut

Hometown: Cornelius, North Carolina

Children: 3

CAREER HIGHLIGHTS

Youngest driver to win a NASCAR Xfinity Series race: 2008

Sunoco Rookie of the Year: 2009

Daytona 500 winner: 2015

NASCAR Cup Series Championship: 2018, 2022, 2024

Named one of NACAR's 75 top drivers: 2023

GLOSSARY

competitive Wanting to be the best.

debut The first time a person performs in public.

drift A technique where a race car driver moves the car sideways.

Legends Race cars that look like 1930s and 1940s American cars but are ⅝-scale.

mentor A person who helps another to be their best.

NASCAR National Association for Stock Car Auto Racing.

Victory Lane The place where a race winner goes after winning.

READ MORE

Bylenga, Heather Rook. **NASCAR Racing.** Mendota Heights, MN: North Star Editions, 2023.

Koestler-Grack, Rachel A. **Stock Cars.** Mankato, MN: Amicus, 2023.

Ventura, Marne. **STEM in the Daytona 500.** Minneapolis, MN: Abdo Publishing Co., 2020.

ON THE WEB

Joey Logano
https://joeylogano.com/

NASCAR Kids
https://www.nascarkids.com/

INDEX

About the Author

Mary Bleckwehl is a children's author who loves cookie dough and talking to kids. She is happiest when she is biking and exploring new places. Mary lives in Minnesota with her husband and monster dog. Check out her books at marybleckwehl.com.